Rosemary Hellyer-Jones

The Adventures of King Arthur
and his Knights of the Round Table

Ernst Klett Verlag
Stuttgart · Leipzig

Contents

Before you read 4

  1 Storm in the night 6
  2 The sword in the stone 7
  3 The new king 10
  4 The broken sword 14
  5 Excalibur 17
  6 The Round Table 19
  7 The knight with the strange face 22
  8 Sir Gawain and the Green Knight 25
  9 The Green Chapel 27
10 The last seat – and a new quest 32

Activities 37
Solutions 45
Names and places in the story 48

Before you read

1. *Look at the picture on the front of the book. Describe it as well as you can. Some of the words in the list below will be useful.*

2. *What do you already know about King Arthur?*

3. *Can you answer these questions? Look at the words here again – and the pictures – for help.*

   a) *How does a man's name "change" when he becomes a knight? (This happens today, too!)*
   b) *What does the King (or Queen) do when he (or she) "knights" a man?*
   c) *Why do you think it was important for Arthur and his knights to sit at a "Round Table"?*
   d) *What did knights wear (and carry!) at jousting tournaments?*

---

knight [naɪt] Ritter
to knight [naɪt] zum Ritter schlagen
Sir [sə] Sir (Anrede für einen Ritter)
armour [ˈɑːmə] Rüstung
weapon [ˈwepən] Waffe
sword [sɔːd] Schwert
lance [lɑːns] Lanze

to joust [dʒaʊst] mit Lanzen kämpfen
tournament [ˈtʊənəmənt] Turnier
the Round Table [raʊnd ˈteɪbl] Tafelrunde, runder Tisch
crown [kraʊn] Krone
cloak [kləʊk] Umhang

---

4. *Now look at the list of names and places in the story (p. 48). Have you heard of any of them? If so, what do you know?*

Chapter 1: Storm in the night

Our story begins on a wild winter's night, many centuries ago. Our scene is the South West of Britain. On that January night there was a terrible storm. All around the coast of Cornwall the storm raged. Great waves ran up the beaches
5 and crashed onto the rocks. At Tintagel, where there are high, rocky cliffs, the wind was wild and the sea was black and angry. But it could not reach the great castle at the top of the cliffs.

There was a secret cliff path that came down from
10 Tintagel Castle. And on that path, against the wind and the rain, a tall man in a long black cloak was moving through the night. He was carrying a bundle in his arms. The tide was coming in fast now, and there was no time to lose. The bottom of the path ran between rocks, and at high tide the
15 sea came up over it. Now, with the bundle warm and safe

4 **to rage** [reɪdʒ] wüten, toben • 6 **cliff** [klɪf] Klippe • 7 **to reach** [riːtʃ] erreichen • 11 **cloak** [kləʊk] Umhang • 12 **bundle** [ˈbʌndl] Bündel • 12 **tide** [taɪd] Flut

inside his cloak, the man jumped over the wet rocks just before the waves could get to him.

He had a long way in front of him. It was many miles to the castle in the Wild Forest near Wales, where he was taking the baby in his arms.

Up in the highest tower of Tintagel Castle, there was a light still in the window. Queen Igrayne sat at that window in the candlelight. She was crying. Her husband Uther, High King of Britain, took her hand in his, but his own heart was so heavy, he could find no words to say.

Chapter 2: The sword in the stone

"But Father! Arthur is only fifteen. He's too young to come with us to the tournament," said Kay. "He'll only get in the way. He isn't even a knight yet!"

"But I can be your squire, Kay," said Arthur quickly. "I'll look after the horses, and I'll polish your armour." Then he looked at Sir Ector. "Please, Father! Say I can come! You know how much I want to."

Sir Ector smiled to see Arthur's excited young face. "All right, Arthur. It'll be a good chance for you to see what a real tournament is like. You'll be useful too, I'm sure."

Kay said nothing, but he didn't look pleased, Arthur saw. He was older than Arthur and he had become a knight just a few weeks before. Now, finally, he was allowed to fight in his first tournament – with his father and other knights of the land. Why should Arthur, still only a young boy, be allowed to go with them?

• • •

---

4 **forest** ['fɒrɪst] Wald • 8 **husband** ['hʌzbənd] Ehemann • **sword** [sɔːd] Schwert • **stone** [stəʊn] Stein • 12 **tournament** ['tʊənəmənt] Turnier • 14 **squire** [skwaɪə] *hier:* Knappe (Diener eines Ritters) • 15 **to polish** ['pɒlɪʃ] polieren • 15 **armour** ['ɑːmə] Rüstung • 18 **all right** [ɔːl 'raɪt] in Ordnung, also gut

Crowds of people were on the road to London. Knights on horseback with their squires, lords and their ladies. Farmers, people with lots of money in their pockets, others with nothing. Everybody was on their way to the tournament – to take part in it, or only to watch.

Late in the afternoon, when Sir Ector and his two boys arrived in town at last, they were lucky to find a room. The Blue Ball Inn had only one left. After their evening meal, Arthur got up from his chair first. He was tired after the long ride and went upstairs to bed.

"Have a last glass of wine with me, Kay," said Sir Ector when Arthur had gone. He looked at his son. "I haven't told you this yet," he said quietly, "but there is something very special about the tournament here in London tomorrow."

"Special? What do you mean, Father?"

"The Archbishop has organized it – because we have to find a new king."

"Find a new king? I don't understand."

"As you know, Kay, Britain is without a High King. When King Uther died thirteen years ago, there was nobody to follow him. Then the minor kings and the lords began to fight against each other. Because they all wanted to be the High King themselves. Soon the Saxons, our old enemies, saw their chance and started to invade parts of the kingdom. The fighting all these years has been terrible!"

Kay listened carefully as his father went on. "Well, there was a big surprise here in London last Christmas. Many of the greatest knights and lords were in town. And when they came out of the Cathedral after Mass on Christmas Day, they saw something very strange. Outside the Cathedral, in the middle of the square, there was a great big stone.

---

2 on horseback [ɒn ˈhɔːsbæk] zu Ross • **5 to take part in s.th.** [teɪk ˈpɑːt] an etwas teilnehmen • **8 inn** [ɪn] Gasthaus, Herberge • **8 left** [left] *hier:* übrig • **16 archbishop** [ˌɑːtʃˈbɪʃəp] Erzbischof • **21 minor** [ˈmaɪnə] *hier:* geringer • **24 to invade** [ɪnˈveɪd] eindringen in • **25 kingdom** [ˈkɪŋdəm] Königreich • **29 cathedral** [kəˈθiːdrl] Kathedrale • **29 mass** [mæs] Heilige Messe • **31 middle** [mɪdl] Mitte

And in the middle of the stone was the handle of a great sword. When they went nearer, they could see these words on the stone in beautiful gold letters:

THE ONE WHO PULLS THIS SWORD OUT OF THIS STONE IS THE TRUE KING OF BRITAIN.

Well, you can imagine what happened then! The knights and lords went crazy! They pushed each other out of the way to get to the stone. Everyone tried to pull the sword out. One after the other. But not one of them could move it."

"And then?" Kay said.

"Then, suddenly, a strange old man appeared at the front of the crowd. It was Merlin, the old wizard from Wales."

"Merlin? I've heard of him!" said Kay. "He's the one who can see into the future – or so people say."

"Yes, that's him. Well, he stood in front of the people and said, 'Our true king is not here yet. But he will come! And then there will be a miracle.' And he asked the Archbishop to organize a big tournament for the beginning of February – so all the knights of the land could be there for it!"

"And this is it!" said Kay. "So will I have the chance to try, too, Father? To pull the sword out? Now I'm a knight, too?"

"Yes, I think so," said his father slowly. "After the tournament everyone will be able to have a try."

---

1 **handle** ['hændl] Griff • 4 **to pull** [pʊl] ziehen • 5 **true** [truː] wahr • 12 **to appear** [əˈpɪə] erscheinen • 13 **wizard** [ˈwɪzəd] Zauberer • 19 **miracle** [ˈmɪrəkl] Wunder

Chapter 3: The new king

The field for the great tournament was outside the walls of London town. Sir Ector and the two boys were riding towards it when Kay suddenly stopped his horse. "Father! I've forgotten my sword!" he cried. "We'll have to go back."

5 "But we'll miss the beginning of the tournament if we go back now," said Sir Ector.

"I'll ride back to the inn and get it for you, Kay," said Arthur. "I'm your squire, so it's my fault really. It was my job to get your weapons together, but I didn't think –"

10 "Silly boy!" said Kay. "Well, ride off as fast as you can now!" So Arthur turned his horse around and rode back to the town. But when he arrived at the Blue Ball, he found that the inn was closed. There was nobody there. Everybody was at the tournament, of course.

15 "What can I do?" thought Arthur. "People will laugh at Kay if they see him at the tournament without his sword. And he'll be angry with me if I go back without it."

Unhappy and worried, Arthur went back to his horse. He rode through the empty streets for a few minutes and
20 tried to think of a plan. And then, suddenly, there he was in the big square in front of the Cathedral. When he saw the great sword in the stone, at first he couldn't believe his eyes. What a stroke of luck! The gold letters shone in the sun, but Arthur didn't even notice them.

25 "Just what I was looking for!" he cried, jumped off his horse and ran over to the stone. Nobody was guarding it. The square was as empty as the streets. So nobody saw Arthur as he took the handle of the sword in his hands and pulled.

---

1 **wall** [wɔːl] *hier:* (Stadt-)Mauer • 3 **towards (s.th.)** [təˈwɔːdz] auf (etwas) zu •
5 **to miss** [mɪs] *hier:* verpassen • 8 **It's my fault** [fɔːlt] Es ist meine Schuld •
24 **to notice** [ˈnəʊtɪs] bemerken • 26 **to guard** [gɑːd] bewachen

The sword came out of the stone at once. Easily and quietly. And for a quick moment, with the winter sun on his face, Arthur felt something like music in his blood.

• • •

"But this isn't my sword, Arthur –" Kay began angrily.

"Sorry, Kay, it's the best I could do," said Arthur. "I couldn't get into the inn, so –"

"Give it to me!" Kay shouted suddenly. Now he recognized the great sword. He took it from Arthur roughly and ran over to Sir Ector. "Father, look! The sword from the stone! I've got it!"

Sir Ector looked at him. But the boy's eyes did not meet his father's. "How did you get this?" he asked Kay quietly.

"I – I went out last night – and pulled it out of the stone. I –"

"Kay, I think we'll have to go back to the Cathedral." He looked over his shoulder at the younger boy. "You, too, Arthur," he called. "We'll miss the tournament, but never mind!"

So they all rode back, and soon they were in the square outside the Cathedral.

"Show me how you did this, Kay," said Sir Ector. "First put the sword back into the stone." But Kay couldn't do it. He tried to push it in, but it was impossible. He turned his face away from his father.

"No more lies, now, Kay!" said Sir Ector in a quiet voice. "Tell me how you got the sword."

"Arthur gave it to me," Kay whispered.

"What's all the trouble?" said Arthur. He took the sword from Kay. "Look, it's easy!"

And he pushed the sword back into the stone. Then, with a quick, easy movement of the right hand, he pulled it out again. "There! What's so difficult about that?"

---

8 **to recognize** [ˈrekəgnaɪz] erkennen • 9 **roughly** [ˈrʌfli] grob, ruppig •
23 **impossible** [ɪmˈpɒsəbl] unmöglich • 27 **to whisper** [ˈwɪspə] flüstern •
31 **movement** [ˈmuːvmənt] Bewegung

But when he looked at Sir Ector and Kay, he couldn't believe his eyes. They were down on their knees in front of him. The strange feeling of music in his blood was with him again for a moment. But he didn't know what it meant.
5 "Father! Kay! Why are you on your knees? I –"
"Arthur, you are our King," said Sir Ector. "The miracle has happened!"
"King?" said Arthur. "But how? How can *I* be King?"

That evening the Cathedral square was full of people.
10 All the knights from the tournament were there, and the Archbishop was there, too. The sword was back in the stone now. One after the other, the knights tried to pull it out again. But nobody was able to move it. Then, as the sun went down behind the houses, a tall man in a black
15 cloak appeared from the crowd. He went and stood at the Archbishop's side.
"It's Merlin!" Sir Ector whispered to Kay.

"People of Britain! Good knights!" cried Merlin. "One stormy night, fifteen years ago, I took a little baby to Sir Ector and his wife. To their castle in the Wild Forest, near Wales. I told them to look after the child as their own son – and to call him Arthur."

Arthur looked at Sir Ector. "Father! Is this true?"

Sir Ector nodded.

"So I'm not your son? And all these years I thought –"

"That little child," Merlin went on, "was the son of King Uther and Queen Igrayne. I took him away from them because his life was in danger at the Court. But I promised to make him King when the time was right. King Uther had many enemies and – as you all know – one of them poisoned him thirteen years ago. But little Arthur was safe in his new home. His new mother and father were good to him."

Sir Ector put his arm around Arthur's shoulders. "Oh Arthur, dear boy! I've always loved you as my own son. But now the time has come –"

"Arthur!" called the Archbishop. "Come up to the stone now, and show that you are our King!"

"What? That boy?" someone called out. "He won't be able to move that great sword! Never!"

"Wait and see," said someone else. "The Archbishop must know what he's talking about,"

Everyone went quiet when Arthur took the handle of the sword. Then, as easily as a warm knife through butter, the wonderful sword came out of the stone. At once there were loud cheers on every side.

"Arthur! King Arthur!" called the knights. "Long live the new King!"

The Archbishop, with Merlin at his side, took Arthur into the Cathedral, and all the people followed. There, in

---

11 **court** [kɔːt] *hier:* Hof, Königshof • 14 **to poison** [ˈpɔɪzn] vergiften • 29 **cheer** [tʃɪə] Jubelruf

the light of hundreds of candles, the Archbishop knighted Arthur, and put the crown of Britain on his head.

"Speak to them, Arthur," whispered Merlin.

So Arthur, with that music in his blood again, spoke to the knights and all the people: "Now I am your King – and I will serve you well. Together we will fight against the Saxons and win back our land. Together we will stand for everything that is good, for everything that is true. Give me your hearts, people of Britain, and I will give you mine. As long as I live, I will serve you!"

Chapter 4: The broken sword

From the day when Arthur became King, Merlin was always there to help and advise him, just as he had always been with King Uther, years before. And Arthur's new army fought and won battle after battle – against the Saxons and against other enemies from Scotland and Ireland. Then Arthur built great castles to defend the coasts and borders of the kingdom. One of these castles was at Caerleon in South Wales. But Arthur's favourite castle, where he had his Court, was Camelot. It was the most beautiful castle in all the kingdom.

One day Arthur heard news of a strange knight, a very strong man called Sir Pellinore. Pellinore had his tent at the side of the road to Camelot, and every time people rode along that way, Pellinore stopped them. They had to fight against him – or go a different way.

"He's a terrible man!" said Gryflet, a young squire at Arthur's Court. "A lot of people have fought against him – but not one of them was strong enough. So far he's killed them all!"

---

1 to knight [naɪt] zum Ritter schlagen • **2 crown** [kraʊn] Krone • **6 to serve** [sɜːv] dienen • **16 to defend** [dɪˈfend] verteidigen • **16 border** [ˈbɔːdə] Grenze • **22 tent** [tent] Zelt • **28 so far** [səʊ ˈfɑː] bis jetzt, bisher

"This must stop," said Arthur. "He's a bully – nothing else!"

"My lord! Let *me* go and stop him!" said Gryflet, on his knees now in front of the King. "Let me have the chance to fight!"

"No, Gryflet, you're too young," said Arthur. "You'll have no chance against Pellinore. He's too big and strong."

But Gryflet gave Arthur no peace, until finally Arthur said, "All right, Gryflet, I won't stop you. You are a brave young man. Come! I will knight you now, before you go. But you must promise one thing. Just go and joust with Pellinore once. Then come back here to Camelot."

Gryflet was overjoyed. He put on his armour, got his weapons together and rode away. But only a short time later, his horse arrived back at Camelot; the boy was lying on the horse's back, with an awful wound in his side. Merlin shook his head. "That was your mistake, Arthur. The boy was too young."

"Pellinore will pay for this!" shouted Arthur. And in no time he was on his horse.

In a terrible rage, he rode to Pellinore's tent. A great big man with long red hair under his helmet was sitting there by the roadside.

"Defend yourself, Pellinore!" shouted Arthur. "You great bully!" His voice was loud and strong, but he could see that this man was much bigger than he was himself.

"Who are you then?" said Pellinore, and he got on his great horse and picked up his lance.

"Arthur, High King of Britain!"

Pellinore looked pleased. "The one with the famous army? Great! I was planning to join you, Arthur – to be one of your knights. Come on, we needn't fight. Let me explain –"

---

8 peace [piːs] Ruhe, Frieden • **9 brave** [breɪv] tapfer, mutig • **11 to joust** [dʒaʊst] mit Lanzen kämpfen • **13 overjoyed** [ˌəʊvəˈdʒɔɪd] überglücklich • **15 to lie, lay, lain** [laɪ] liegen • **16 wound** [wuːnd] Wunde • **23 lance** [lɑːns] Lanze

"You stop people on the road to my castle. You have wounded my youngest knight! So you must die!" And Arthur got his horse ready to charge.

The two men jousted three times. They charged towards each other and their lances clashed together. The third time Pellinore used his lance with great force – and knocked Arthur off his horse.

"You're better than me at jousting, I see!" shouted Arthur. "But let's see how well you can fight on foot. Come on! Get off your horse!"

As a knight, Pellinore had to follow the rules. So he jumped down from his horse, and the two men went at each other with their swords. Arthur had the wonderful sword from the stone. He felt safe with that in his hands! Nothing could hurt him, he was sure. But Pellinore's sword was stronger than Arthur thought.

The forest echoed with the sound of the two swords as they clashed together. The two men fought long and hard, and soon their blood was on the grass. Arthur's body was hurting everywhere, but he didn't give up. Then – quite suddenly – Arthur's sword broke.

"Aha!" Pellinore cried out in triumph. "Give up, Arthur – or die!"

"Never!" answered Arthur. But in a moment Pellinore had him on the ground, pulled his helmet off his head – and raised his sword, ready to kill the King.

"Pellinore!" There was a cry from behind the trees.

And then, without warning, the enormous man fell to the ground and closed his eyes. Arthur couldn't believe it. What had happened?

"Don't worry, Arthur. Pellinore cannot hurt you now. He is sleeping."

---

3 **to charge** [tʃɑːdʒ] stürmen, angreifen • 5 **to clash** [klæʃ] klirrend aneinander schlagen • 6 **force** [fɔːs] *hier:* Wucht • 7 **to knock (off)** [nɒk 'ɒf] hinunterstoßen (von) • 17 **to echo** [ˈekəʊ] hallen • 22 **triumph** [ˈtraɪəmf] Triumph • 26 **to raise** [reɪz] erheben • 28 **enormous** [ɪˈnɔːməs] riesig, groß

And there – just behind him – stood the tall figure of Merlin.

"He was too strong for me!" cried Arthur, and there were tears in his eyes. "And look at my sword! Broken already! What does it mean, Merlin? Are my days as King at an end already?"

"Of course not," said Merlin. "There was no magic in the sword itself. It was only a symbol. – And Pellinore here, he is strong, as you have seen. A bit stupid – but that will change. In time he will be one of your finest knights, Arthur. – Now, come with me, and we will get you a new sword. One that will never break."

But Arthur's eyes were closing. He had lost a lot of blood. He tried to answer Merlin, but no words came.

Chapter 5: Excalibur

When Arthur's eyes opened again, it was evening and he was in a place he did not recognize. In front of him there was a beautiful lake. The clear water was like a mirror, it was so calm. Tall forest trees grew around the sides of the lake, as quiet as ghosts. There was no wind in the trees, and no birds were singing. In the west, the sun had gone down behind the blue hills, and a soft gold light lay over the quiet water.

"Is this a dream?" Arthur whispered. "What is this place?"

"Lake Avalon," Merlin answered. "Climb into the boat, Arthur."

A small boat was at the side of the water. Arthur had not seen it at first. As if he was walking in a dream, Arthur went

---

1 figure ['fɪgə] Gestalt • **4 tears** [tɪəz] Tränen • **8 symbol** ['sɪmbl] Symbol • **9 stupid** ['stjuːpɪd] dumm, blöd • **17 mirror** ['mɪrə] Spiegel • **21 soft** [sɒft] weich • **28 as if** [əz 'ɪf] als ob

to it and climbed in. A moment later, the boat began to move slowly over the water.

"Look, Arthur! The sword!" called Merlin behind him.

And there, in the middle of the lake, Arthur saw
5 something very strange. A beautiful gold sword, in a sheath with jewels on it, was slowly appearing out of the water. The sword was shining in the evening light, and as Arthur came nearer, he saw that a white hand – with a woman's fingers – was holding it. Was someone holding it
10 out to him?

Take it, the hand seemed to say. *It is for you.*

So Arthur took the sword, and at once the white hand sank back into the water. Slowly the boat brought him back to where Merlin was waiting for him.

15 "The name of the sword is Excalibur," Merlin told him as he stepped out of the boat. "Always keep it with you, Arthur. It will serve you in many battles. But the magic is not only in the sword itself. Look at the sheath! Feel it!"

---

6 sheath [ʃiːθ] Scheide • **6 jewel** [ˈdʒuːəl] Edelstein, Juwel • **13 to sink, sank, sunk** [sɪŋk] sinken • **16 to step** [step] steigen, gehen

And when Arthur ran his fingers over the jewels on the sheath, he felt the magic. His body suddenly became strong again, and in a moment all the pain from his wounds left him.

"If you always have the sheath with you," Merlin said, "no wound will kill you, no poison will work on you. Nobody – nothing – will be able to hurt you."

"But who …?" Arthur whispered. "Who gave me the sword? It was a lady's hand! But whose?"

"It was the Lady of the Lake," answered Merlin. "One day, when all your work is finished, Arthur, and your time as King is over, Excalibur must go back to her. But it will be many years before that moment comes."

Chapter 6: The Round Table

"Are you quite sure, Arthur?" Merlin looked at the King. "There are many other beautiful ladies in the land …"

"But no lady as beautiful as Guinevere! She will be the perfect Queen. As soon as I saw her, I knew she was the one!"

Merlin smiled. "I see you are in love with her. But –"

"And why not?" said Arthur. "Don't you think I have chosen right?"

"It is impossible to be sure," answered Merlin slowly. "Time will tell. – Of course, she is a lovely lady. And a princess. So, if you have decided …"

"I have!" said Arthur. He was twenty now, and it was time for him to choose a Queen.

• • •

---

12 over [ˈəʊvə] vorbei • **round** [raʊnd] rund • **23 time will tell** [ˌtaɪm wɪl ˈtel] es wird sich noch herausstellen • **23 lovely** [ˈlʌvli] reizend, schön

All the knights and ladies in the kingdom had invitations to the wedding. Arthur brought his new bride to Camelot, and there was a big feast for them and their guests. When they entered the Great Hall of the castle, there was a surprise for them. Merlin was standing there – in front of an enormous round table.

"Welcome, King Arthur and Queen Guinevere!" the wizard cried. "Here is your wedding present from the bride's father. The most beautiful table in Britain. Soon the most famous in the world!"

• • •

All kinds of wonderful food were on the table, ready for the feast. Roast beef and chicken, different kinds of fish. Vegetables from the castle gardens. Big gold plates with the finest fruit. Cakes, bread, puddings, sweets. And the best wines, red and white.

But, in comparison with the table itself, the food was nothing. It was a huge round table, made of oak, and around it there were seats for a hundred and fifty people! The King and his new Queen walked around the table and looked at the beautiful seats. They saw that there was a name on the back of each seat. Some of the names were of knights that Arthur knew: SIR ECTOR, SIR KAY, SIR GAWAIN, SIR GRYFLET, SIR PELLINORE … But others he did not recognize yet at all: SIR LANCELOT, SIR PERCIVAL …

"These men will be your knights some time in the future," Merlin explained. "And when a knight dies, his name will slowly disappear – and then another name will appear in its place."

"My name still looks clear enough!" laughed Arthur as he touched the back of his own seat. Then he saw a seat

---

2 **wedding** ['wedɪŋ] Hochzeit • 2 **bride** [braɪd] Braut • 3 **feast** [fi:st] Festessen, Bankett • 3 **guest** [gest] Gast • 12 **roast beef** [rəʊst 'bi:f] Rinderbraten (aus dem Backofen) • 14 **pudding** ['pʊdɪŋ] kuchenartiger Nachtisch • 17 **huge** [hju:dʒ] sehr groß, riesig • 17 **oak** [əʊk] Eiche • 28 **to disappear** [ˌdɪsə'pɪə] verschwinden • 31 **to touch** [tʌtʃ] anfassen, berühren

with no name on it at all. "And who is this seat for?" he asked Merlin.

"This is the Dangerous Seat. It is for the best and truest knight in the world. He is not here yet. But if the wrong person tries to sit here, he will die at once."

"Well, how will we know who the best knight is?" Arthur asked.

"When the time is right, you will know," said Merlin.

Then Arthur spoke to all the knights. "In the past, there were sometimes arguments between you. Often one knight wanted to be more important than another. This table will put an end to these arguments. From this day you will be called the Knights of the Round Table. You will be the bravest knights in the world. You will fight for each other – and for the good of all. The stories of your great adventures will live forever. Now take your cups, and we will drink to the future."

---

3 **the truest** ['truːɪst] *hier:* der treueste …, der beständigste … • 15 **the good of all** [ˌɡʊd əv 'ɔːl] das Gemeinwohl • 16 **forever** [fəˈrevə] für immer • 16 **cup** [kʌp] *hier:* Becher

"To the future! To our good King! To King Arthur and Queen Guinevere!" the knights cried, their cups full of wine.

"To all the Knights of the Round Table!" cried Merlin. And then, slowly and quietly, the old wizard disappeared.

Chapter 7: The knight with the strange face

Next year, the day before Easter, when Arthur and his knights were having supper in the Great Hall, one of the King's squires came up to him. "A stranger is here, my lord," he said. "He is asking to speak to you."

"Bring him in!" said Arthur.

So the squire brought the stranger in. He was a tall young man with black hair. All the knights looked at him as he went down on his knees in front of the King. "How ugly he is!" Sir Kay whispered to the knight next to him. "Look at his face!"

The young man certainly had a strange face. One side was different from the other, and the right corner of his mouth was higher than the left. But, as Arthur noticed at once, his grey eyes were true and steady.

"Tell me your name," said Arthur, "and why you have come to Camelot."

"My name is Lancelot," said the young man. "Son of King Ban, who once fought at your side. I have heard so much about you that I, too, would like to be one of your knights. Now Merlin, the great wizard, has sent me to you."

"You are welcome here, Lancelot!" said the King in a warm voice. "I'll knight you tomorrow – on Easter morning!"

• • •

---

6 **Easter** ['iːstə] Ostern • 7 **supper** ['sʌpə] Abendessen • 8 **stranger** ['streɪndʒə] Fremder • 14 **ugly** ['ʌgli] hässlich • 16 **certainly** ['sɜːtnli] gewiss • 19 **steady** [stedi:] *hier:* ruhig, fest

The next day, when the King knighted Lancelot, two ladies of the Court fastened his new spurs for him. Queen Guinevere stood next to them. She had decided to fasten his new belt herself. She wanted to be kind to him, because she had heard what some of the knights were saying about him behind his back. "He's so ugly," one of them had laughed, "he certainly won't find a lady at this Court who wants him as her champion!"

Now, as she fastened the young man's belt, Guinevere looked up into his face. Lancelot's steady grey eyes looked down into her own. For a moment, time seemed to stand still. The Queen looked away again quickly, but it was a moment she never forgot.

• • •

For the next few days, a number of the other knights grumbled to each other about Lancelot. Especially Sir Kay. "Why should he become a knight so easily?" he said. "Nobody knows him at all! He just comes here and introduces himself to the King – and the next day he has a place at the Round Table like the rest of us!"

Lancelot knew what they were thinking, but he tried to take no notice.

One evening, when Sir Gawain and the King were playing chess together by the fire, Lancelot found that he could not keep his eyes away from Queen Guinevere. She was sitting by the fire, too, and she looked very beautiful in the soft light.

"She's a lovely woman, isn't she?" said Lionel, Lancelot's squire, so quietly that only his lord could hear. "What a pity that she is the Queen!"

---

2 **to fasten** ['fɑːsn] befestigen • 2 **spurs** [spɜːz] Sporen • 4 **belt** [belt] Gürtel, Waffengürtel • 8 **champion** ['tʃæmpiən] Kämpfer; Ritter, der sich fur eine besondere Sache/eine besondere Dame einsetzt • 15 **to grumble** ['grʌmbl] murren, klagen • 8 **to introduce oneself** [ˌɪntrə'djuːs] sich vorstellen • 23 **chess** [tʃes] Schach • 28 **What a pity!** [ˌwɒt ə 'pɪti] Wie schade!

The next morning, Lancelot talked to Arthur. "Let me go on a quest, my lord," he said. "I want to show that I am a worthy knight of your Court."

"Don't listen to Kay and the others, Lancelot," said Arthur. "Even as a boy, Kay was always jealous. That's just the way he is."

"I don't care what Kay thinks of me," answered Lancelot. "I just want to be sure *myself* that I am worthy to be a Knight of the Round Table."

So Arthur let Lancelot go. And he and his squire Lionel had many adventures. They fought against King Arthur's enemies. They even had battles with monsters and dragons. No other knight in the kingdom was braver than Lancelot.

• • •

A year had gone by and yellow cowslips were in the fields again when Lancelot rode back to Camelot. Everyone had heard about his great adventures, and it was a proud moment for him when he came into the Great Hall, saw the King, and went down on his knees.

"Well done, Sir Lancelot!" said Arthur. "You have shown time and time again how worthy you are to be a Knight of Camelot. And you are still so young – only nineteen!"

When Lancelot looked up, he saw that the Queen was there, too. She looked more beautiful than ever, and her eyes shone like gold lights. And at that moment Lancelot knew something that made his heart very heavy. His feelings for Guinevere were the same as before, if not even stronger. She was the love of his life. Nothing could change that. But she was also the wife of his dear King.

---

1 to go on a quest [ˌɡəʊ ˌɒn ə 'kwest] auf ritterliche Abenteuersuche gehen • **3 worthy** ['wɜːði] würdig • **5 That's just the way he is** [ðæts dʒəst ðə ˌweɪ hi 'ɪz] So ist er eben. • **13 dragon** ['drægn] Drachen • **15 cowslip** ['kaʊslɪp] Schlüsselblume

Chapter 8: Sir Gawain and the Green Knight

Of all the knights' many adventures, Sir Gawain's adventure with the Green Knight was one of the strangest. It all began on New Year's Eve – at the time when Sir Lancelot was still away. King Arthur and his knights were sitting at the Round Table, and all the ladies and squires were in the Great Hall, too. Everyone was talking and laughing. Just before the great feast began, the big doors at the end of the hall opened with a crash – and a man on horseback rode in.

A sea of faces turned to look at the stranger. He was enormous. The knights had never seen a man so tall – or a horse so huge. But the most fantastic thing about this figure was the colour. Everything about him was green. His clothes, jacket, boots, all these were a brilliant green. His long hair and his beard were as green as the oak trees in summer, and his face and hands were green. In one hand he held a huge axe. It was green, too. Even his horse was green. The Court had never seen anything like it.

"Who is the lord of this castle, then?" the Green Knight shouted in a voice like thunder. There was no answer. "Have you all lost your tongues?"

"I am the lord here," said Arthur finally. "I am King Arthur."

"Ah! King Arthur! I've heard a lot about you and your famous knights," said the Green Knight. "And now I have a challenge for you! A test! To check how brave you really are …"

"No problem," answered Arthur. "I'm sure one of my good knights here will joust with you, if that is what you want."

---

3 **New Year's Eve** [ˌnjuː ˌjɪəz 'iːv] Silvester • 14 **boot** [buːt] Stiefel • 15 **beard** [bɪəd] Bart • 17 **axe** [æks] Axt • 19 **Lord** [lɔːd] *hier:* Herr • 21 **tongue** [tʌŋ] Zunge • 26 **challenge** ['tʃælɪndʒ] Herausforderung

"No!" shouted the strange knight. "Not one of these men here is strong enough to fight against *me*!" He looked around the Court.

"No, the challenge is a different one. I will give my axe to one of your knights. He will be your champion against me. And then he can use my axe – it is the best axe in the world, and the sharpest – to strike me one blow. But only one! Don't worry, I won't move! I will take the blow as well as I can. But your champion must promise one thing. On New Year's Eve next year I will be allowed to return that blow."

The knights looked at each other in silence.

"What a crazy idea!" said Arthur.

The Green Knight laughed. "Cowards! There's not one brave man at this Court! And you call yourselves knights? Pah!"

He turned his horse and moved towards the great doors.

"Wait!" called a voice. It was Sir Gawain. "Give me the axe. I'll take up the challenge! I swear I'll only strike one blow. And next year you can do the same to me!"

It was a strange scene. The Green Knight got off his horse, gave the green axe to Sir Gawain, and went down on his knees in front of him. He bent his head, and Sir Gawain raised the axe.

There was an awful silence as Sir Gawain waited for a moment with the axe in the air. Then, with all his strength, he brought the axe down. It was so heavy and so sharp that it cut straight through the Green Knight's neck. His huge green head fell to the floor. There was blood everywhere. But the knight did not fall. He stood up, picked up his head by its green hair, and climbed back onto his horse.

---

7 sharp [ʃɑːp] scharf • **7 to strike s.o. a blow** [straɪk ə ˈbləʊ] jdm. einen Schlag versetzen • **10 to return (a blow)** [rɪˈtɜːn] *hier:* zurückschlagen • **12 silence** [ˈsaɪləns] Stille, Stillschweigen • **14 coward** [ˈkaʊəd] Feigling • **19 to swear, swore, sworn** [sweə, swɔː, swɔːn] schwören • **23 to bend, bent, bent** [bend, bent, bent] biegen; *hier:* neigen • **26 strength** [strenθ] Kraft, Stärke • **28 neck** [nek] Hals, Nacken

"Don't forget your promise!" came a voice from the Green Knight's head. "Next New Year's Eve – at the Green Chapel, in the forest north of Wales!"

And with his green head still in his hand, the terrible figure rode out into the cold, dark night.

Chapter 9: The Green Chapel

The months went quickly. When the trees in the forest were turning yellow, Sir Gawain left Camelot and started on his way north. He had no idea where the Green Chapel was. For many days he rode through the border country of Wales. Wherever he stopped for the night, he asked people the way to the Green Chapel, but nobody was able to tell him. The weather got colder and winter came. He was north of Wales now. Finally, tired and sad, he came to a beautiful castle. It was Christmas Eve.

---

3 **chapel** [tʃæpl] Kapelle • 5 **dark** [dɑːk] dunkel • 7 **to turn** [tɜːn] *hier:* werden • 14 **Christmas Eve** [ˌkrɪsməsˈiːv] Heiligabend

The lord of the castle gave Sir Gawain a warm welcome. "We don't often have guests," he said. "Stay with us as long as you like."

Gawain was glad to stay, he was so tired after his long journey. "But I must leave before the end of the year," he said. "I've promised to be at the Green Chapel on New Year's Eve – and I haven't even found out where it is yet."

"The Green Chapel?" said the lord. "It's only a few miles from here."

Gawain was pleased. He was dreading his meeting with the Green Knight, but at least he could try to enjoy these last few days at the castle. The lord was very friendly, and his wife was glad to have a guest, too.

A few days after Christmas, the lord said, "I'm going to hunt in the forest tomorrow. My wife will look after you here. And I have an idea for a little game. In the evening, when I come home, we'll exchange whatever we got during the day."

Gawain had no idea what the lord meant, but he agreed.

• • •

Next morning, at breakfast time, the lord had already gone. His wife, a very beautiful woman, sat with Gawain at the table. She moved her chair nearer to his, and began to flirt with him.

"Here we are, alone together at last!" she cried. "Aren't you going to take me in your arms? There's nobody here to see us!"

Gawain found her fascinating, but she was his new friend's wife. And, of course, he wanted to be a worthy Knight of the Round Table.

"What a strange knight you are!" she said. "Aren't you even going to ask me for a kiss?"

---

10 **to dread s.th.** [drɛd] große Angst vor etwas haben, mit Schrecken an etwas denken • 15 **to hunt** [hʌnt] jagen; auf die Jagd gehen • 17 **whatever** [wɒtˈevə] was auch immer • 23 **to flirt** [flɜːt] flirten • 24 **at last** [ət ˈlɑːst] endlich • 27 **fascinating** [ˈfæsɪneɪtɪŋ] faszinierend • 31 **to ask for s.th.** [ɑːsk] um etwas bitten

"If that really is what you want –" Gawain began. "All right, I will ask for a kiss. But only one!"

So she gave him a kiss, smiled, and left the room.

• • •

When the lord came home, he gave Gawain the deer he had killed in the forest. And in exchange, Gawain put his arms around him and gave him a kiss on the cheek.

"Is that what you got today?" the lord asked with a laugh. Gawain nodded.

"Ah! Where did you get it from?"

"I won't tell you that," said Gawain. "That isn't part of the game."

• • •

The next day the same thing happened. The lady of the castle flirted with Gawain again, and again she gave him a kiss. In the evening, the lord gave Gawain three rabbits he had killed. And in exchange, Gawain gave him another kiss.

• • •

On the third morning, Gawain woke up from a terrible nightmare about the Green Knight. It was December the thirtieth, the last day before the awful meeting. Just as he was getting up, the lady of the castle came into his bedroom. She was wearing a beautiful dress with a lovely green sash.

"Your last day with me!" she said, and gave him a kiss. "I'll be so sad when you leave."

She put her arms around him, but he said, "Remember your husband, dear lady!"

"Such a worthy knight!" she said. "Well, at least let me give you a present before you leave." And she took off the

---

4 **deer** [dɪə] Hirsch, Reh, Rotwild • 6 **cheek** [tʃiːk] Wange, Backe • 18 **nightmare** ['naɪtmeə] Alptraum • 22 **sash** [sæʃ] Schärpe (Gürtel aus Stoff) • 27 **such** [sʌtʃ] solch, so

green sash. "Take it! But don't tell my husband. It's a magic sash! If you wear it, nobody can kill you."

At once Gawain thought of the Green Knight. He took the sash, and she gave him another kiss.

That evening, Gawain gave the lord two kisses, but he said nothing about the sash.

• • •

Next morning, Gawain left the castle early. The lord had told him the way to the Green Chapel, and with a heavy heart he rode down the path through a dark valley. After a few miles, he suddenly heard a strange noise. What could it be? And then he knew. His heart stood still. Somebody was sharpening an axe!

This part of the valley was very green – even in winter. On the right of the path, there was a cave in the rock, with green moss all around the sides. Could this be the Green Chapel?

"Come out, Green Knight!" called Gawain. "I am here!"

There was silence, then suddenly the Green Knight appeared at the mouth of the cave. Taller, stronger, even more terrible than Gawain had remembered.

"Welcome!" he cried. "Now take off your helmet, Sir Gawain, and get ready for my turn with the axe!"

The moment he had dreaded was here. Down on his knees, Gawain bent his head – and the terrible knight raised the axe. Then, just before the axe came down, Gawain moved his head away – he just could not help it!

The Green Knight laughed. "Scared? You aren't as brave as I thought, Sir Gawain!"

"Strike again!" said Gawain. "I won't move this time, I promise!"

So the great knight raised his axe again. Gawain closed his eyes and fought against his fear. With a crash the axe

---

9 valley [ˈvæli] Tal • **12 to sharpen** [ˈʃɑːpn] schleifen, schärfen, wetzen • **15 moss** [mɒs] Moos • **19 mouth** [maʊθ] *hier:* Eingang • **26 I can't help it** [aɪ ˌkɑːnt ˈhelp ɪt] ich kann nichts dafür, kann nicht anders • **32 fear** [fɪə] Furcht, Angst

came down, but it just missed Gawain's head. He heard it as it cut into the earth near his right ear.

The Green Knight laughed. "Braver this time, I see! I was just testing you!"

"Testing me? Stop this game!" cried Gawain. "Strike the blow properly now – but this is your last chance!"

For the third time the Green Knight raised his axe. When he brought it down, it hit Gawain, but made only a small wound on the side of his neck. Not much more than a scratch. Gawain jumped up in triumph, and looked the Green Knight in the face. The Green Knight smiled – and suddenly Gawain recognized him. It was the lord of the castle, in his green hunting clothes! He looked smaller now. Slowly the green colour faded from his face.

"But how …? Why …?" Gawain was speechless.

"I have tested you – and found you are a true knight!" said the lord. "I never wanted to kill you! The first two blows were for the kisses from my wife. And the third blow was for the sash. I gave you a small wound for that, because you kept it for yourself!"

Gawain looked down at his feet. "So you knew …?"

"I knew everything! And I knew why you took the sash. But that was only a small fault, Gawain. It's only natural for a young man to love his own life. – Keep the sash, Gawain. It will bring you luck – and keep you safe on your way back to Camelot."

Gawain looked at him in wonder. "But who are you? How can you change into a green man? And how can you lose your head – and not die?"

"My name is Sir Bertilak. But I cannot tell you more. Only remember this, Sir Gawain. When you meet magic in our strange times, you must not ask too many questions."

---

6 **properly** ['prɒpəli] richtig, korrekt • 10 **scratch** [skrætʃ] Kratzer • 14 **to fade** [feɪd] verbleichen, verschwinden • 15 **speechless** ['spiːtʃləs] sprachlos • 23 **fault** [fɔːlt] *hier:* Fehler • 23 **natural** ['nætʃrəl] natürlich • 27 **in wonder** ['wʌndə] staunend

Chapter 10: The last seat – and a new quest

Years passed. Many new knights came to Camelot and took their seats at the Round Table. Sir Bedevere, the knight who stayed at Arthur's side till the end of his life. Sir Percival, the country boy from Wales who left home and became a knight when he was only sixteen. Sir Gareth, Gawain's younger brother. And many more. But still the Dangerous Seat, where nobody dared to sit, was empty.

One bright afternoon in June, one of Arthur's squires ran into the castle with strange news.

"Come down to the river and see what I've found!" he cried. "There's a stone – with a great sword in it!"

The younger knights had never seen anything so strange. Arthur looked at the great red stone in the river that ran past Camelot, and he remembered that day in London so long ago.

"Merlin must have something to do with this," he said quietly.

"What a beautiful sword!" cried Sir Gareth. "And look! There are letters on the stone!"

The knights came closer, and Lancelot read out the words:

> THE ONE WHO CAN PULL THIS SWORD FROM THIS STONE IS THE TRUEST KNIGHT IN THE WORLD.

"It can't be me," said Gawain sadly, and he touched the green sash that he always wore.

All the knights looked at Lancelot, the knight who had been a hero in so many adventures. But it could not be him, he knew that. His love for Queen Guinevere was as

---

7 to dare [deə] wagen • **8 bright** [braɪt] leuchtend, hell • **20 to read out** [riːd ˈaʊt] (laut) vorlesen

strong as ever. The King's wife! No, *he* could not be the truest knight ….

• • •

That evening, at supper time, two visitors arrived at Camelot. A nun came into the Great Hall, and at her side was a tall young man. She introduced him to King Arthur.

"This is Galahad. His mother died when he was still a baby, and Merlin brought him to our convent, where we looked after him all these years. Now the time has come for the boy to become a knight."

When the knights and ladies looked at Galahad, they seemed to recognize him. But they did not know why. Lancelot knew. When he looked at the boy's face, he saw his own grey eyes. And the fair hair – Galahad's mother's hair had been like that! His poor mother, Lady Elaine …

"Welcome to Camelot, Galahad," said the King.

"Welcome, dear boy," said Lancelot. "So you are here at last! I am Lancelot."

Galahad looked him straight in the eyes, and smiled. "Father!" he said quietly. So the nuns at the convent had told him. Lancelot was glad.

"I see there's a place for me at the table!" said Galahad, and he walked straight up to the Dangerous Seat.

"Not there! Don't sit there!" all the knights cried. "If the wrong person sits in that seat – !"

Lancelot tried to pull the boy away. But it was too late. Galahad had already sat down. And nothing had happened. Nothing at all. The knights could not believe it!

"He's all right! It's a miracle!"

When they looked at the back of the seat, they saw that a new name had appeared – in bright gold letters: SIR GALAHAD.

---

4 **nun** [nʌn] Nonne • 8 **convent** [ˈkɒnvənt] (Frauen-)Kloster • 14 **fair** [feə] *hier:* blond, hell

"But he's not a knight yet, is he?" said Sir Bedevere.

"Down to the river, everybody!" cried Arthur. "Your sword is there, Galahad, and I'm going to knight you with it!"

• • •

5 It was a great moment for young Galahad. One by one, the other knights had all shown they could not pull the sword from the red stone. Now it was his turn. The water came up over his boots as he stepped into the river. He took the handle of the sword – and out it came. Quickly and easily.
10 When he heard the loud cheers all around him, he looked around and laughed, the beautiful sword in his hand.

And there were tears in Arthur's eyes when he knighted him.

So the Round Table was now complete. Late that night,
15 the whole Court sat together in the Great Hall, with the last plates of a great feast still in front of them. Lancelot

---

5 one by one [wʌn baɪ ˈwʌn] einzeln, einer nach dem anderen

looked at young Sir Galahad and remembered that night, years ago now, when Lady Elaine had tricked him. She had loved him with all her heart, and had wanted to marry him, but he had only loved Queen Guinevere. So Elaine and her father had tried to trick Lancelot into love for her. One evening her father had feasted long with him, and poured the sweetest wine into his cup. Then, in the dark night, Elaine had come to him and pretended that she was Guinevere. And Lancelot, his head heavy with wine, had fallen for the trick. Next morning, when he saw the mistake he had made, it had been too late. So – from this strange mistake, this trick – a child had come into the world. Later, when the child was still a baby, Lady Elaine had died – of a broken heart. The father of her son had never loved her!

Lancelot looked at the Queen. She smiled at him and they both knew: even after so many years, their silent love for each other was still as strong as ever.

Then, quite suddenly, the doors of the Great Hall opened – but no one came in.

"The wind! It's the wind!" cried the knights as all the candles went out. Through the dark room, a wonderful perfume began to spread, sweeter than a field of summer flowers. Everyone was silent as a strange, small light came into the room. Although the light was small, it was so white and pure, so very beautiful, that everyone looked at it in wonder. Brighter than the brightest star they had ever seen in the night sky. As it came slowly through the air, closer to the Round Table, the knights saw what it was. But not one of them could speak – they could only look at the miracle in front of their eyes: it was the Holy Grail.

---

2 **to trick** [trɪk] hereinlegen, mit einer List betrügen • 6 **to feast** [fiːst] *hier:* beim Festessen sitzen • 7 **to pour** [pɔː] einschenken, eingießen • 8 **to pretend** [prɪˈtend] vortäuschen, so tun als ob • 10 **to fall for a trick** [ˌfɔːl fərˌə ˈtrɪk] auf einen Trick hereinfallen • 16 **silent** [ˈsaɪlənt] still: *hier:* unausgesprochen • 22 **perfume** [ˈpɜːfjuːm] Parfüm, Duft • 22 **to spread** [spred] sich ausbreiten • 25 **pure** [pjʊə] rein, makellos • 30 **the Holy Grail** [ˌhəʊli ˈɡraɪl] der Heilige Gral

A pure white cloth covered the cup, so they could not see the full wonder of it. But they all knew in their hearts that this was the 'Cup of cups' – the cup of the Last Supper.

Then suddenly, when everyone had seen it and recognized it, the Holy Grail disappeared.

"A sign from God," said Arthur quietly.

"For a new quest!" said Gawain, and he jumped up from his seat. "Tomorrow I will ride out into the world and look for the Holy Grail. When I have found it and seen it in its full wonder, then – and only then – I will come back to Camelot!"

"We will all look for it!" said Lancelot.

"I swear I will see it uncovered before I die!" cried Galahad.

"Then go, all of you, with my blessing!" said Arthur. "Only God knows what wonders there will be, what miracles you will see."

And so the Quest for the Holy Grail began. All the knights rode out from Camelot, and each one went his own, different way. In front of them lay all kinds of adventures. There are so many stories that nobody has ever been able to tell them all. And although Arthur's days as High King of Britain were over long ago, the magic of Camelot and of the Knights of the Round Table still lives on. Some even say it will live on for ever.

THE END

---

1 cloth [klɒθ] Tuch • **1 to cover** [ˈkʌvə] bedecken • **3 the Last Supper** [lɑːst ˈsʌpə] das (Letzte) Abendmahl • **13 uncovered** [ʌnˌkʌvəd] enthüllt • **15 blessing** [ˈblesɪŋ] Segen

Activities

1 Storm in the night

1. *Is this right? If you find a mistake, correct it.*

   a) Tintagel Castle is on the coast of Cornwall.

   b) On the night when the story begins, the weather is good and the sea is calm.

   c) The man who is coming down the cliff path is carrying a baby in his arms.

   d) He must be as quick as he can because someone is following him.

   e) King Uther and Queen Igrayne are feeling very sad.

2. *Think about it: The man in the black cloak must have a reason for what he is doing. What might that reason be? Can you guess?*

2 The sword in the stone

1. *Arthur wants to go to the tournament in London with Sir Ector and Kay. But Kay doesn't like the idea. Why not?*

2. *At the Blue Ball Inn, Sir Ector talks to Kay about King Uther. What do we find out about him – and about Britain in the years since he died?*

3. *Sir Ector also talks to Kay about a strange stone and a sword. What does he tell him?*

4. *How does Kay react when he hears about the sword?*

3 The new king

1. *Can you complete the sentences?*

    a) Arthur rides back to the inn because …

    b) But he can't get in because …

    c) He knows people will laugh at Kay if …

    d) When Arthur rides into the Cathedral square, he sees …

    e) When he takes the handle of the sword and pulls, …

2. *What lie does Kay tell his father? Why do you think Kay does this?*

3. *How does Arthur feel when he pulls the sword out of the stone? And why is he so surprised?*

4. *How do you think Arthur feels that evening, when Merlin speaks to the people?*

5. *What a day! Imagine: When Arthur goes to bed that night, he thinks about all the strange things that happened. Write down your ideas.*

    Start like this:
    "What a day it's been! I was so worried when I couldn't get into the inn … But when I saw that wonderful sword in the stone …"

4 The broken sword

Which is right?

1. *Sir Pellinore is a bully because*
   a) he kills Gryflet ☐
   b) he stops people on the way to Camelot ☐
   c) he fights against Arthur ☐

2. *Arthur's sword breaks when*
   a) he is jousting with Pellinore ☐
   b) Pellinore knocks him off his horse ☐
   c) the two men are fighting on foot ☐

3. *There are tears in Arthur's eyes because*
   a) he wasn't as strong as Pellinore ☐
   b) he needs a better sword ☐
   c) he is so glad that Merlin is there to help him ☐

4 *Pellinore*
   a) must die because he wanted to kill the King ☐
   b) is too stupid to become a good knight ☐
   c) will be one of the Knights of the Round Table some time later ☐

5 Excalibur

1. *What is the name of …*

    a) the place where Merlin takes Arthur after the fight with Pellinore?

    _____

    b) the beautiful sword with jewels on its sheath?

    _____

    c) the person who gives Arthur the new sword?

    _____

2. *What is so special about the new sword and its sheath? How can they help Arthur?*

6 The Round Table

Imagine you are one of the guest at Arthur's wedding. Later, a friend asks you some questions. How would you answer them?

1. "What was there to eat and drink at the wedding?"

2. "I heard one of the presents was a big table. Who was it from? And what is it like?"

3. "Is there a special seat for Arthur? Or are all the seats the same?"

4. "What's so special about a *round* table? Did anyone say anything about it?"

7 The knight with the strange face

1. *What does Lancelot look like? Why has he come to Camelot?*

2. *What new things does he get when he becomes a knight?*

3. *Talk about what the characters in this chapter think and/or feel – in these situations:*

   a) Arthur, when he looks into Lancelot's eyes.

   b) Sir Kay, when he first sees Lancelot.

   c) Queen Guinevere, when Lancelot is knighted.

   d) Sir Kay, during the next few days.

   e) Lancelot, when the King is playing chess with Sir Gawain.

   f) Lionel, when he notices that Lancelot is looking at the Queen.

   g) Lancelot, when he talks to Arthur the next day.

   h) Lancelot, when he comes back to Camelot a year later and sees the Queen.

8 Sir Gawain and the Green Knight

1. *Can you re-tell the story with these sentence parts? Match the beginning of each sentence (1–11) with the correct ending below (a–k).*

   Example: 1. The story begins on New Year's Eve, when …
       d) everyone was sitting in the Great Hall.

   1. The story begins on New Year's Eve, <u>when</u> …
   2. <u>Before</u> they had started eating, …
   3. The man was enormously tall, <u>and</u> …
   4. The strangest thing about the man was <u>that</u> …
   5. He had a challenge for Arthur and his men, <u>but</u> …
   6. His idea was to give his axe to one of them, <u>and</u> …
   7. Then, in a year's time, the day would come <u>when</u> …
   8. <u>Although</u> he knew the idea was crazy, …
   9. So the Green Knight went down on his knees, <u>and</u> …
   10. <u>After</u> he had lost his head, …
   11. <u>When</u> he got back on his horse, …

   a) it was the Green Knight's chance to return the blow.
   b) he rode away with his head in his hand.
   c) Sir Gawain cut through his neck with the axe.
   d) everyone was sitting in the Great Hall.
   e) his horse was very big, too.
   f) the Green Knight picked it up by its hair.
   g) a man rode in through the hall doors.
   h) he didn't want to joust with any of them.
   i) all his clothes – and even face and hands – were green.
   j) Sir Gawain agreed to take up the challenge.
   k) this knight would be allowed to strike him one blow.

2. *Did you enjoy this Chapter? Talk about it with a partner, or in groups. These words may give you some ideas.*

9 The Green Chapel

1. *Who says this? Who to?/What is the situation?*

    a) "Stay with us as long as you like."

    b) "I have an idea for a little game."

    c) "What a strange knight you are!"

    d) "That isn't part of the game."

    e) "It's a magic sash!"

    f) "Scared? You aren't as brave as I thought!"

    g) "Stop this game!"

    h) "When you meet magic, you must not ask too many questions."

2. *What – or who – does this describe? Page numbers are given if you need to look at the text again.*

    a) turning yellow (p. 27)

    b) tired and sad (p. 27)

    c) very beautiful (p. 28)

    d) lovely green (page 29)

    e) taller, stronger, even more terrible … (p. 30)

3. *Imagine! You are Sir Gawain. How do you describe your adventure when you get back to Camelot?*

10 The last seat – and a new quest

1. *Which description goes with which person?*

   a) Galahad's mother;
   b) Sir Gawain's brother;
   c) the lady Lancelot loves;
   d) the "truest knight in the world";
   e) Galahad's father;
   f) the country boy from Wales;
   g) the High King of Britain;
   h) the knight who was with Arthur till the end;
   i) the wizard from Wales.

   Bedevere
   Arthur
   Galahad
   Lady Elaine
   Lancelot
   Gareth
   Percival
   Merlin
   Guinevere

2. *How…*

   a) does Lancelot guess that Galahad is his son?
   b) does Galahad know who Lancelot is?
   c) can the knights be sure that Galahad is the right person for the Dangerous Seat?
   d) does Galahad show that he is the "truest knight"?
   e) does Lancelot feel when he looks at the Queen?
   f) do the knights get the idea for a new quest?

Solutions

Before you read

1. King Arthur is standing in front of a beautiful old castle. He is wearing a dark red cloak, and there is a gold crown on his head. In his right hand he is holding a sword, in his left a helmet.
2. *individual answers*
3. a) When a man becomes a knight, he is called 'Sir' (e.g. Sir Lancelot, Sir Paul McCartney!).   b) The King/Queen takes a sword and holds it over the man's left shoulder. (Before he is knighted, the man goes down on his knees in front of the King/Queen.)   c) The Round Table shows that no knight is more important than another.   d) They wore amour, and they carried a lance.
4. *Individual answers*

Activities

1 Storm in the night

1. a) Right.   b) Wrong! On that night there is a terrible storm, and the sea is black and angry, with big waves.   c) Right.   d) He must be quick because the tide is coming in, and he has to jump over the wet rocks at the bottom of the path.   e) Right.
2. It might be that he wants to save the baby from danger.

2 The sword in the stone

1. Kay thinks Arthur (15) is too young to go to the tournament. Kay has just become a knight and wants to enjoy the tournament without the younger boy.
2. After King Uther died (13 years ago/before), other men wanted to be the High King, and fought against each other. Then the Saxons started to invade the kingdom.
3. On Christmas Day people saw a great stone with a sword in it, in front of the Cathedral. Gold letters said: 'The person who pulls the sword out of the stone is the true King.'
4. He wants to have the chance to try to pull it out of the stone himself.

3 The new king
1. a) ... Kay has forgotten his sword / has left his sword there.
   b) ... the inn is closed.   c) ... they see him at the tournament without his sword / a sword.   d) ... the sword in the stone.
   e) ... the sword comes out at once.
2. He says he pulled the sword out of the stone during the night. He says this because he would like to be King himself.
3. He feels 'music in his blood'. He is surprised when he sees Sir Ector and Kay on their knees.
4. He must feel very surprised (that Sir Ector isn't his father!), and very excited that he is now the new king.
5. *individual answers*

4 The broken sword
1. b)   2. c)   3. a)   4. c)

5 Excalibur
1. a) Lake Avalon   b) Excalibur   c) The Lady of the Lake
2. There is magic in the sword and in the sheath. No wound or poison can hurt Arthur if he has the sheath with him.

6 The Round Table
1. "There was beef, chicken and fish. And there were vegetables and fruit, bread, cakes, sweets and wine."
2. "The table was from the bride's father. It's a very, very big oak table."
3. "There's a special seat for each knight, and a special seat for Arthur, too, but one seat has no name on it."
4. "Arthur explained this. No knight is more important than another knight. So nobody sits in a 'higher' place at a round table!"

7 The knight with the strange face
1. He is tall and young, and has black hair. But he has a strange face, with one side different from the other. He wants to become one of the knights.
2. He gets spurs and a new belt.
3. a) Arthur sees from Lancelot's eyes that he is true and steady.   b) Sir Kay thinks Lancelot looks ugly.   c) Queen Guinevere feels this is a very special moment ...   d) Sir Kay

feels jealous.   e) Lancelot thinks how beautiful Guinevere looks.   f) Lionel thinks Lancelot is in love with the Queen.   g) Lancelot feels he wants to be a worthy knight.   h) Lancelot's heart is heavy because he still loves the Queen.

8   Sir Gawain and the Green Knight
1. 1 d)   2 g)   3 e)   4 i)   5 h)   6 k)   7 a)   8 j)   9 c)   10 f)   11 b)
2. *individual answers*

9   The Green Chapel
1. a) The lord of the castle says this to Sir Gawain when he arrives on Christmas Eve.   b) The lord of the castle, to Sir Gawain, the day before he goes hunting.   c) The lord's wife, to Gawain, when he doesn't take her in his arms.
   d) Gawain, to the lord, when the lord asks who the kiss was from.   e) The lady, to Gawain, when she gives him her sash on the last day.   f) the Green Knight, to Gawain, when he moves his head away from the axe.   g) Gawain, to the Green Knight, when he tells Gawain: "I was just testing you!"
   h) The lord of the castle, to Gawain, when he asks questions about all the strange things that have happened.
2. a) the trees in the forest (in autumn)   b) Sir Gawain (on Christmas Eve)   c) the lord's wife   d) the sash on the lady's dress   e) the Green Knight (at the mouth of the cave / the Green Chapel)
3. *individual answers*

10   The last seat – and a new quest
1. a) Lady Elaine   b) Gareth   c) Guinevere   d) Galahad   e) Lancelot   f) Percival   g) Arthur   h) Bedevere   i) Merlin
2. a) Galahad's grey eyes are like his own eyes, and his hair is fair like his mother's.   b) The nuns at the convent have told him.   c) Galahad doesn't die when he sits there.   d) He pulls the sword out of the stone in the river.   e) He knows that their love for each other is still strong.   f) They get the idea when they see the light of the Holy Grail in the Great Hall at Camelot. They only see it for a moment, then it disappears. This moment is very special for them all.

Names and places in the story

King Arthur ['ɑːθə]
Queen Igrayne [ɪ'greɪn]
King Uther ['juːθə]
Sir Kay [keɪ]
Sir Ector ['ektə]
Merlin ['mɜːlɪn]
Sir Pellinore ['pelɪnɔː]
Sir Gryflet ['grɪflət]
The Lady of the Lake [ˌleɪdi əv ðə 'leɪk]
Sir Gawain [gʌ'weɪn]
Queen Guinevere ['gwɪnɪvɪə]
Sir Lancelot ['lɑːnsəlɒt]
Sir Percival ['pɜːsɪvəl]
King Ban [bæn]
Lionel ['laɪənəl]
The Green Knight [ˌgriːn 'naɪt]
Sir Bertilak ['bɜːtɪlæk]
Sir Bedevere ['bedɪvɪə]
Sir Gareth ['gærəθ]
Sir Galahad ['gæləhæd]
Lady Elaine [ˌleɪdɪ ɪ'leɪn]

Caerleon [kɑː'liːən]
Camelot ['kæmɪlɒt]
Lake Avalon [ˌleɪk 'ævəlɒn]
Tintagel Castle [tɪn'tædʒl 'kɑːsl]

Excalibur [ɪk'skælɪbə]